FEB -- '04

THE
RENAISSANCE

MARY QUIGLEY

Heinemann Library
Chicago, Illinois

© 2003 Heinemann Library
a division of Reed Elsevier Inc.
Chicago, Illinois

Customer Service 888-454-2279

Visit our website at www.heinemannlibrary.com

Map illustrations by John Fleck
Color illustrations by Marty Martinez
Photo research by Amor Montes de Oca
Printed and bound in the United States by Lake Book Manufacturing, Inc.

07 06 05 04 03
10 9 8 7 6 5 4 3 2 1

Library of Congress Cataloging-in-Publication Data
Quigley, Mary.
  The Renaissance / Mary Quigley.
     p. cm. -- (Understanding people in the past)
Summary: Presents an overview of the history of European society during
the time known as the Renaissance, from the fourteenth to the
seventeenth century.
Includes bibliographical references and index.
  ISBN 1-4034-0388-0 (HC), 1-4034-0608-1 (Pbk.)
  1. Renaissance--Juvenile literature. 2.
Europe--Civilization--Juvenile literature. 3.
Europe--History--476-1492--Juvenile literature. 4.
Europe--History--1492-1648--Juvenile literature. [1. Renaissance. 2.
Europe--Civilization.] I. Title. II. Series.
  CB361 .Q34 2002
                    2002002349

Acknowledgments
The author and publisher are grateful to the following for permission to reproduce copyright material:
Title page, pp. 4, 5T, 11, 13, 15, 16, 21, 22, 24, 32, 34, 39B, 40, 41T, 42, 43T, 44, 45L, 46, 47, 50B, 51T 52T, 54 The
Granger Collection; p. 5B Francesco Venturi/Corbis; pp. 6T, 39T, 41B, 45C, 51B, 53 Bettmann/Corbis; p. 7T Scala/Art
Resource; p. 7B David Lees/Corbis; p. 8 Sandro Vannini/Corbis; p. 9 Vittoriano Rastelli/Corbis; p. 10 Todd
Gipstein/Corbis; p. 12T Nik Wheeler/Corbis; p. 12B The Bridgeman Art Library, New York; p. 14 Elio Ciol/Corbis; pp.
17, 19, 37, 43B, 45R, 55 North Wind Pictures; p. 18 Ludovic Maisant/Corbis; p. 20 Joanna Booth/The Bridgeman Art
Library, New York; pp. 23, 29T Gianni Dagli Orti/Corbis; p. 25T Giraudon/The Bridgeman Art Library, New York; p.
25B Jim Zuckerman/Corbis; p. 26 Alexander Burkatowski/Corbis; p. 27T James L. Amos/Corbis; p. 27B Philadelphia
Museum of Art/Corbis; pp. 28, 33, 38, 56B Archivo Iconografico, S. A./Corbis; p. 29B Erich Lessing/Art Resource;
 p. 30 Peter Harholdt/Corbis; p. 31T Francis G. Mayer/Corbis; p. 35T Geoffrey Clements/Corbis; p. 35B North Carolina
Museum of Art/Corbis; p. 36 Historical Picture Archive/Corbis; p. 49 Werner H. Miller/Corbis; p. 50T Charles & Josette
Lenars/Corbis; p. 52B Victoria & Albert Museum, London/Art Resource; p. 56T Araldo de Luca/Corbis; p. 57
Philadelphia Museum of Art/Corbis; p. 58 David Reed/Corbis; p. 59 Charles E. Rotkin/Corbis

Cover photograph: The Granger Collection

Some words are shown in bold, **like this.** You can find out what they
mean by looking in the glossary.

Contents

People in the Renaissance

The Renaissance was a special time in the history of Europe. It began at the end of the **Middle Ages** and lasted from the fourteenth to the seventeenth century. During this time, the people of Europe were swept up in an amazing flurry of creativity. Artists were painting **murals**—such as *The Last Supper* and the ceiling of the Sistine Chapel in Rome—that are still famous today. They were also creating sculptures in marble that were unlike anything else. New ideas were printed in books and more people learned to read. Breakthrough discoveries were made in science. People came to have a more accurate view of the world.

In the Renaissance, even doors became a place to display beauty. This bronze panel was created by Lorenzo Ghiberti.

Renaissance means "rebirth." The people of the Renaissance felt reborn. Things had begun to change for them. A **plague** that had killed one-fourth to one-third of the people in Europe was in the past. The **feudal system,** which allowed a few wealthy landowners to control most of the population, was becoming outdated. The poor farmers who had been bound to the land of the wealthy were asking for more rights and trying new trades.

Art during the Renaissance reflected an appreciation for ancient **mythology,** as seen in this painting by Sandro Botticelli.

A new start

Europe became less rural during the Renaissance. It was filled with busy towns and cities. A new type of citizen emerged in these towns and cities and a **middle class** formed. People living at this time were inspired by the rediscovery of Greek and Roman languages, art, philosophy, and literature.

The artist Michelangelo was probably present when this **classic** sculpture of Laocoon was unearthed.

Laocoon

Laocoon is the person in Greek mythology who tried to warn the people of Troy not to bring a wooden horse, offered as a gift from the Greeks with whom they were at war, into the city. The people did not follow his advice, brought the horse into the city, and found it was filled with soldiers. This famous sculpture (right) portrays Laocoon and his sons being killed by sea serpents. The people of Troy had mistakenly assumed that the death of Laocoon was a sign from the gods that he could not be trusted.

The Renaissance Ideal

The Renaissance began in the early 1300s in Italy. That was where many of the lost treasures of the **Roman Empire** were found. Italy was the center of **trade**, art, and ideas. The Renaissance soon spread to France, England, Germany, and Spain.

The Renaissance man

The ideal Renaissance man would be well-educated and articulate. He could carry conversations with anyone. He would be able to defend himself, and his fellow citizens. He would be a **diplomat**. He would also be strong and good looking. But this was not enough, he would need to be good at many

A Renaissance man had to be good at many things. Leonardo da Vinci is a perfect example of a Renaissance man—he was a painter, inventor, and scientist.

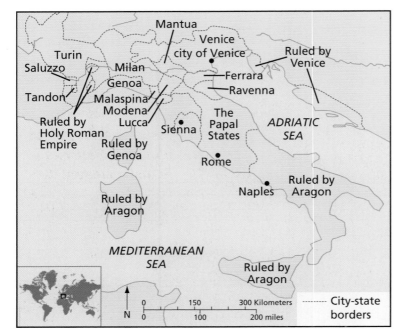

The Renaissance began in Italy in the early 1300s. At that time, Italy was not a united country as it is today. Instead, it was composed of many **city-states,** all competing with each other.

things, such as sports, art, and science. The Renaissance man had to be everything.

Still divisions

Not everyone experienced the Renaissance in the same way. People lived very differently depending upon their wealth, status, and gender. Despite this, the quality of life improved for many. People lived better and so they lived longer than in the past. Also, though new ideas were exciting, they were also considered dangerous by those who feared change.

Not everyone felt the positive force of the Renaissance. Poverty was still a very real part of life.

Michelangelo went back to sign his famous sculpture, the *Pieta*, so that people would believe he actually created it.

The Renaissance did not happen very long ago, so we know a lot about it. No **archaeological excavation** is necessary to find its treasures. Evidence of the Renaissance can be seen in the buildings that still stand in Europe and the huge number of art pieces from the time period.

Art

The paintings and sculpture from the Renaissance tell us what was important and beautiful to people at that time. We know that they thought the human body was beautiful because it became the subject of their art. We also know that they found beauty in nature, as can be seen in their landscape painting. Renaissance art shows the importance of **realism** and honesty to the artist, because they worked hard to make their sculptures and paintings look exactly like the real thing.

The Vatican is the home of the Catholic Church. It holds many treasures created during the Renaissance that visitors can see.

New ideas

Just as artists were learning to carefully study the world around them, those interested in science and **theology** looked closely at the ideas handed down to them. They looked for ideas that seemed incorrect, or that did not make sense.

Restoration

Professional **restorers** can use computer programs and microscopes to analyze damaged Renaissance art. Using special video cameras, they can see beneath the layers of paint to study the artist's original sketches. They can also analyze the paints to determine how old a painting is. They use their artistic skills to make art look like it used to.

Repairing and preserving art is a very important job that requires patience and skill. This painter is restoring a **fresco** in the Sistine Chapel.

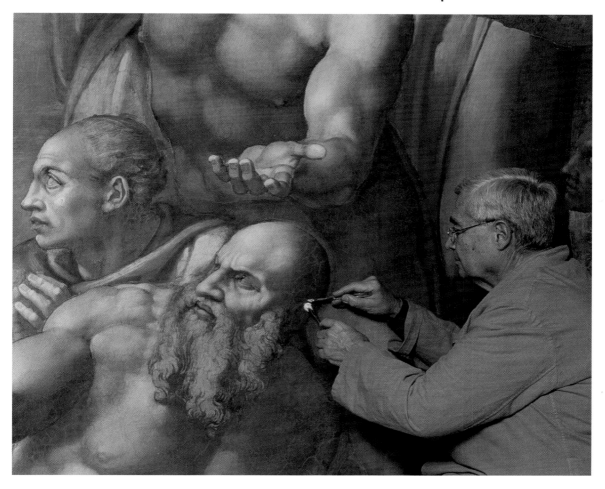

Art and architecture

Art museums around the world have examples of Renaissance art. There are also many reproductions of famous Renaissance art pieces that decorate homes and churches. Some art and architecture of Europe was created by the most famous Renaissance artists and architects of the world. Much of this is part of the everyday landscape of modern Europe.

Globes

Globes created during the Renaissance show how explorers delivered important information to mapmakers. At the beginning of the Renaissance, many countries were not known and were missing from the globe. Exploration changed that.

People often go to museums to see Renaissance artwork like these paintings by Peter Paul Rubens, located in the Louvre in Paris.

There are about 48 copies of the Gutenberg Bible, which was created by Johannes Gutenberg on the printing press he invented during the Renaissance.

Medicine

The Renaissance was the beginning of a new era in medicine. Doctors began to study the human body in new ways. They had artists help them make careful drawings of the body. They soon learned that the human body was much different on the inside than they had envisioned.

Writings

Leonardo da Vinci's notebooks have survived, though in scattered pages and incomplete volumes. The work of Chaucer and Shakespeare, both Renaissance authors, is preserved in books that students still read copies of in school today.

The Renaissance city

During the Renaissance, **democratic** governments emerged in the larger cities. People identified themselves by the city from which they came. For example, people were called Milanese if they were from the city of Milan. They were called Florentine if they were from Florence. There was intense rivalry between cities.

A wealthy and ambitious person could hold a high place in the government of some **city-states**. City-states were governments that were based locally. Many cities of the Renaissance functioned much like

The Medici family became dukes of Florence after building a successful banking business. Except for two brief periods, the Medici family ruled all of Florence from 1434–1737. Their gardens were a favorite place for artists to come and practice their skills by copying the sculptures displayed there.

FIORENZA

The people of Florence, and in other cities, were very proud of where they lived and tried to make improvements to the buildings and streets.

independent nations by creating a distinct **culture,** and by using both diplomacy and war with other powerful cities. Sometimes whole families would dominate local politics.

The Renaissance nation

The Christian lands of western Europe were reunified for a while as the **Holy Roman Empire.** This name showed the increasing influence of the Church in areas that formerly had been part of the Roman Empire. The Catholic Church controlled much of western Europe. Strong city-states tried to maintain independence in their political and business activities. Despite the art and diplomacy of this time, punishment for crimes was often cruel. Religious and political disputes could end with someone dying for what they believed.

Nation-states began to emerge, such as France and England. In England a new family, the Tudors, came to rule. Henry VIII belonged to this family. Queen Elizabeth I, his daughter, was a great monarch. England became powerful in the Renaissance due to navy and military successes against enemies.

Henry VIII was a powerful king of England from 1509 to 1547. He is well known for having had six wives—an usual occurrence during this time.

Rome, Florence, and Venice

Italy is where the Renaissance began. This is because Italians rediscovered their ancient Roman past as they began to find art treasures. They unearthed beautiful sculptures in their homeland, unlike the ones that they were accustomed to. They were amazed by how real the sculptures looked: muscles bulged, hair curled, and faces seemed to show real feelings. Renaissance artists, like Donatello, imitated this realistic style. Once, when he was carving a stone, it looked so real that he pondered that all it needed was to speak.

When Constantinople, capital of the eastern **Roman Empire** fell in 1453 to the **Turks,** many **scholars** fled to Florence and Rome. They brought with them **classical** learning as well as many important Greek books and manuscripts.

Cities such as Rome, Florence, Venice, and others changed as people gained appreciation for beauty. Many artists and poets were born in Florence or spent a lot of time working there. Rome was a bustle of activity, as buildings were extensively rebuilt and remodeled.

Art during the Renaissance was very realistic, as in ancient Roman times. This sculpture of St. Justina was made by Donatello in 1449.

The Turkish invasion of Constantinople drove many classical scholars to Florence and Rome. Once there, they were able to share their knowledge with the people of Italy.

Rome, Venice, and especially Florence were centers for art. As people found a new appreciation for beauty, the skills of artists were in great demand. Cities competed to be the best, and that included having the best sculptures, architecture, and artwork. Cities were rebuilt, as artists and their skills were welcomed. Artists gained great knowledge from the books and manuscripts that scholars from Constantinople had brought to Italy.

In the **Middle Ages,** Catholicism was the main religion. Some people felt that the Catholic Church had strayed from its mission. The Church had become materialistic—spending more time and money on decorating **cathedrals** than tending to people's souls.

Desiderius Erasmus

Desiderius Erasmus was one such person who criticized the Catholic Church. Erasmus was Dutch and traveled widely throughout Europe. He believed that educating people would bring good changes to the Church. By printing and distributing information, he was reaching a population that included more than just **clergy** and **scholars.** He helped make **classical** texts available to the average person.

Erasmus did not want to leave the Catholic Church, but to **reform** it. He believed that **popes** and priests were following their own ambitions and forgetting their duty to follow the scriptures and serve parishioners.

Many Catholic churches were lavishly decorated with sculptures and artwork on the inside and the outside.

Martin Luther

Another person who tried to reform the Catholic Church was Martin Luther, a young German priest and scholar. He saw many things happening in the Church that concerned him. He nailed a list of 95 criticisms of the Catholic Church on a church door. One of his biggest objections was the sale of indulgences. The Catholic Church offered forgiveness of sins and a guarantee of a place in heaven for those who did good deeds. Often, the good deed involved substantial donations to the Church. Luther felt this was wrong. His list of criticisms became known throughout Europe and many agreed with him.

Reformers like Martin Luther tried to make changes in the Catholic Church. When they realized that the Church would not change, most ended up forming their own religions.

Why reform?

People tried to reform the Catholic Church because of the things they felt contradicted biblical teachings, such as the sale of indulgences and the amount of money spent on churches. There was violence over religious differences. When the Catholic Church did not change, Martin Luther and those who followed him formed the **Protestant** branch of Christianity. A new invention, the printing press, helped the Protestant Reformation gain speed and reach more people.

17

Churches and Religion

Churches as patrons

Renaissance churches were often beautiful. In fact, churches competed to be the most beautiful. Church leaders wanted their buildings to be filled with the art that was being created during the Renaissance. Artists relied upon wealthy **patrons** to buy what they made. Sometimes the Catholic Church was their patron. **Popes** and other **clergy** often employed painters, sculptors, and stained glass artists to help decorate their churches.

Patrons usually had very specific ideas of what they wanted done, and they did not always agree with the artists! Leonardo da Vinci was

Stained glass artists created beautiful windows for churches. The windows often depicted scenes from Bible stories.

St. Jerome was a favorite subject for artists. Men were supposed to follow the example of St. Jerome and invest much time in studies and faith.

so annoyed by the monks when he was painting *The Last Supper*, that he painted the face of Judas to look like their **prior.** This would be a big insult to the prior, since Judas betrayed Jesus in the biblical story about the crucifixion.

St. Jerome

Renaissance artists especially enjoyed portraying St. Jerome, who had lived about 1,000 years earlier. He was a good example of Renaissance values. A Renaissance man was expected to know about many things and St. Jerome was a man who studied a lot. Artists frequently portrayed St. Jerome in his study, with volumes of books all around, to promote the value of knowledge. He had brought early Christian writings from Antioch and Bethlehem from which he produced a Bible.

Family Life

Like today

In many ways, children of the Renaissance were like children of today. They played games and they had chores to do. They cared for their younger siblings. There were many things that they needed to learn and much was taught to them at home. Children learned farming skills and how to care for livestock. Girls learned domestic skills, such as sewing and cooking. Formal education was available to children of middle- and upper-class families.

During the Renaissance, parents wanted artists to do portraits and sculptures of their children.

As science advanced and **plagues** subsided, life expectancy increased. More children lived to adulthood. Parents spent more time and money on their children, for what was now a more certain future. Many parents had portraits painted of their children.

Growing up

Children of the Renaissance grew up with many strict rules. Children were often seen as miniature adults, so their clothes were simply smaller copies of adult clothes.

Children did not have many books or games made just for them. The Renaissance world was an adult one. So, children took their place in the adult world at a much younger age. It was common for girls to marry by age fifteen. Men married at young, middle, and old age. Older men usually married a very young wife. Men often remarried after a wife died of disease or during childbirth.

While children were loved by their parents, a lot was expected of them at a very young age. Not much is known about children's actual thoughts and feelings during the Renaissance.

Marriage was an important event. A person's place in a community was often defined by who they married. This painting by Jan Van Eyck is called *The Arnolfini Marriage.*

Renaissance Clothing

Clothing for the rich

Clothing for the wealthy was often elaborate. New dyes and manufacturing techniques meant that more people could dress fashionably. Embroidery on clothing was done in gold and silver. Pearls and gems also decorated the clothes of the wealthy. Wealthy men wore capes made of velvet and other luxury fabrics. They enjoyed wearing bright colors.

Different fabrics and styles

The wealthy tried to maintain a distinction between themselves and everyone else by

Clothes for the wealthy were often similar in design to what poorer people wore, but made with finer material and more decorated.

passing laws that forbade poor and middle income people from wearing certain fabrics and styles. For instance, only **nobles** could wear fur. Fur was readily available and adorned the collars of clothing. Certain clothing might indicate other things besides social class. A gray coat and a red hat indicated that a person had leprosy, a contagious disease. As the **middle class** increased in wealth and influence, these laws were abandoned.

The poor dressed in simple garments made of wool or linen. Their clothes were made to last through hard work.

Functional clothes

The poor dressed simply. Their clothes were made of wool or **linen,** which were more readily available. They had fewer clothes than wealthy people and wore them a long time before washing. The poor dressed for keeping warm, rather than for appearance. Their clothes had to be sturdy enough to last through hard work.

Clothing facts

Wealthy **merchants** often wore turbans dyed red using ground cochineal beetles. Because the dye was expensive, the use of it indicated a person's wealth. Female members of powerful Italian families often had up to 50 gowns, 20 hats, 33 pairs of shoes, and 60 pairs of slippers. A peasant might not even have one change of clothes!

Growing Up and Going to School

New ideas

Most towns had schools where wealthy
children learned reading and writing.
The Renaissance encouraged people to
study in areas that had been forgotten
since **classical** times. **Grammar, rhetoric,** and
history were studied, as well as poetry, art,
and literature. Wealthy Italians thought a
better education would give them an
advantage in their business dealings. Those
who were well-educated were more highly
admired and trusted by others.

The Renaissance was a blend of old and new
ideas. The universities required lengthy study,
as much as seven years. Some students
preferred to move from university to

Universities were open
to anyone who had time
to attend. This
illumination shows a
teacher and students at
the University of Paris.

university, studying what they wanted and then moving along. Every city had its own university. The lessons were open to anybody who had the time to attend. There were no exams. A student could leave school when they were needed at home or when they felt they had learned enough.

Old ways

Wealthy men and boys were encouraged to receive an education at a university. Wealthy women and girls were also educated and often learned music and read many books. The sons of **merchants** might have a **tutor** or go to a school where they would learn a skill or craft. Merchant's daughters might be taught in a **convent.** The poor might be **apprenticed,** but they were often too busy with their daily work to become students. Poor girls often received no education aside from housekeeping and were often married at a young age.

Apprentices learned a skill or craft from someone who was already an expert. The young man sitting in the corner is probably the apprentice at this pharmacy.

Many people went to a monastery or convent to prepare for a religious vocation.

Rural Life and the Farming Year

Living by the season

Although more people were living in cities, many were still farmers. Their work revolved around the seasons. Preparing fields, planting, tending and weeding, and bringing in the harvest were the important events in their year. Likewise, those who worked with livestock followed the cycles of nature, shaving wool from their sheep at just the right time and tending to their animals as they had babies.

Wool was an important product for **trade** and for clothing. On a farm, everyone helped tend and sheer the sheep.

The Tuscan landscape inspired Leonardo da Vinci's appreciation for the beauty of nature. This is a view of Vinci, Leonardo's birthplace.

Country homes

Rural areas attracted more than farmers and their families. It became fashionable for wealthy families to have a home in the country where they could escape the crowds, noise, pollution, and disease of the city. The wealthy often decorated their walls with art showing idealized views of the lives of those who worked the land.

Rural life as art

Nature was an inspiration for art. Landscape art started in the Renaissance. Leonardo da Vinci's earliest known drawing was of the Tuscan landscape. That drawing is said to be the first landscape in western art. Nature was glorified, studied, and imitated. For some, nature was the source of their livelihood. For others, it was an escape from the hectic life of the city.

Painting landscapes became an art form during the Renaissance.

Mix of people

Renaissance cities were usually exciting places. An interesting mix of people would mingle along the streets and in the shops. People exchanged goods, greetings, and ideas. The rich did not avoid the poor, but rather interacted with them, particularly at times when they were sharing food or other things with them in a charitable way.

Building

Whole cities were rebuilt using architectural designs from Greece and Rome. A dome and other structures built by Filippo Brunelleschi were said to have begun the Renaissance in Italy. They gave people an idea of what **classical** architecture could do for the look of a city. The **Pantheon** was the inspiration for the dome. Arches, domes, and pillars were popular features on buildings.

In Venice, waterways flow like streets. People would often get places by boat instead of by walking.

On the street

The streets were a bustle of activity. **Merchants** sold goods from stores or in the marketplace. Craftworkers showed their goods. Artists and merchants made business connections. Cities built new town halls and churches, showing the importance of both government and religion.

The city became a center for commerce, religion, politics, and education. People were more aware of cleanliness and the ways to avoid disease, so gutters were designed to flush away the waste and garbage that people tossed into the streets.

During the Renaissance, people had a lot more goods to choose from while shopping.

The Renaissance marketplace was usually full of activity, as seen in this view of the port and market in Antwerp, Belgium.

Renaissance Homes

New housing styles

During the Renaissance, people wanted more privacy. This is clear from the styles of their homes. Housing styles were simple to spectacular. Families each had separate houses or apartments. Even people with little money had separate bedrooms in their homes for different family members.

Medieval castles were replaced with grand homes without **fortifications.** These homes had large windows made of many small **soldered** panes to let in the sun. Heavy shutters could close out the cold. The use of windows showed that people were not as afraid of attack. It was no longer necessary to stay safely locked behind stone walls in this time of increased civility and diplomacy.

Mansions

The wealthy built mansions called **palazzos.** Artists painted **frescoes** on wet plaster. When the plaster dried, the art was a permanent part of the wall in the palazzo. The homes of the wealthy often had private baths.

During the Renaissance, most people had a minimum amount of furniture and it was usually very useful.

A merchant's home

A city **merchant** would have several rooms in their house and perhaps a shop on one floor. Those who did not have a private bath in their homes went to a public bath.

Homes of the poor

The poor had oiled paper, **parchment,** or canvas windows that were drafty and **opaque.** Their homes might be very small and in poor condition. There would only be some protection from the weather. The invention of the chimney greatly improved homes by releasing the smoke of the fire needed for cooking and warmth outdoors.

In the country, a peasant who was doing well might have a large house made of simple materials. Their homes were built of mud, timber, and thatch. Their farm animals might also share this space.

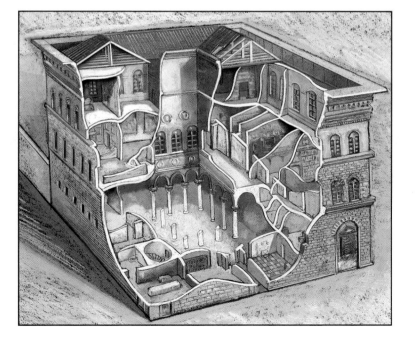

The homes of the wealthy were often very large and beautiful. This house is typical in that it was built around a central courtyard.

Cooking and Eating

As Europeans traveled more and **trade** increased, their diet became more varied. In northern Italy, the woods were full of wild game such as bears, boars, deer, quail, and other birds. The rivers were home to trout and eel. The nearby ocean provided tuna, sardines, lobster, and other seafood.

Pasta

Pasta was a favorite food and was made into special shapes. At first, tomato sauces weren't used. Instead, pasta might be tossed with a cream sauce or olive oil, pine nuts, and herbs.

Soup

Soups with vegetables, beans, meat, and pasta were healthful and filling for those who could obtain the ingredients. Others would eat thin soups made of cabbage and broth.

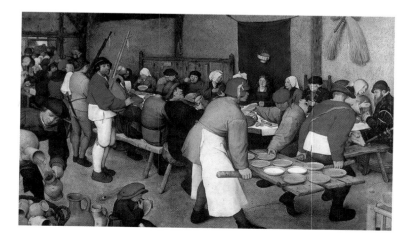

Despite rules of etiquette, such as not spitting at mealtime, a Renaissance dinner might seem chaotic to us today. Forks were only just becoming a common utensil at the dinner table.

You are what you eat

People's diets were influenced by whether they lived in the city or country, how close they were to the ocean, and whether they could readily acquire imported food.

People ate eggs from their chickens and other birds. They drank milk from goats. They used salt, pickling, and drying techniques to preserve foods. Strong spices such as clove, pepper, ginger, and nutmeg were used to cover the taste of rotten food. Food was placed in glazed pottery to make it last longer.

Wine was a common drink. Water was often unsafe to drink, so wine was a safer beverage. Even the poorest people had a few vines of grapes from which they made their own wine.

Sports and Recreation

Music

During the Renaissance, more people were able to afford the luxury of recreation. Even in poor households, there were musical instruments. Music was played for entertainment, rather than only to accompany religious ceremonies.

Games

People had special game tables in their homes. Chess, roulette, **fox and geese,** and **nine men's morris** were some games they played.

Making music became a popular activity in the Renaissance.

In Spain, bullfights were popular. Cards were also popular. Children played games like tag. Collecting was popular in the Renaissance. People often collected fossils, crystals, gems, and preserved animals such as armadillo, crocodile, and even elephant. Illustrated books were also collected.

Falconry was a popular sport. In falconry, a person would accompany a tethered hawk, or other raptor, on its hunt for food.

Like today, people gathered at home for games such as cards and chess.

Crafts and Craftworkers

Guilds

In Florence all citizens could vote or run for office, but to be a citizen one had to be accepted into a **guild.** Being in a guild meant that a person was considered qualified to carry out a certain trade. Each guild had its own emblem. Once accepted into a guild, a person had higher status. Members of guilds participated in local politics to ensure benefits for their skill or trade.

Other crafts

The people of Milan were known for their metalwork. Venice was famous for its glasswork. Some craftworkers gathered,

Silk is a fiber that is turned into thread from which clothes are woven. These women are working in a silk production workshop.

combed, spun, and wove wool. Others worked with a new, popular fabric called silk. People learned how to make silk from the Chinese. A person might be a tailor, vase maker, clock maker, jeweler, or carpenter.

Skills learned by people who made crafts, such as goldsmiths and stonecutters, were applied to the castings and carvings that became famous art. People were needed to use their talents and skills in the building and rebuilding of Renaissance cities. An increased appreciation for art elevated the status of craftworkers, who turned to making things that were not only useful, but beautiful.

The skills of goldsmiths were learned and used by artists who made metal castings.

Banking

During the Renaissance, there was a shift from an **agricultural** to a **commercial** economy. Banking became an important part of society. **Merchants** began acting as lenders. They carried small, precise scales for weighing coins. Any loss of metal decreased the value of the coin.

Merchants and guilds

Renaissance merchants sold their goods at home and abroad, sometimes traveling to North Africa, Asia, and the Middle East. **Guilds** protected the reputation and the concerns of craftworkers. The guilds

Money changers had to keep a close eye on coins to guarantee that none of the valuable metal had been clipped from the edges.

European exports included grain, jewelry, glass, and tapestries. Iron and tin from England, leatherwork from Spain, and cotton and gold thread and spices from the East were popular items of trade.

established guidelines for how one could carry out a particular trade. They set prices and wages. They also collected taxes among their members, provided soldiers in times of war, and sometimes took part in city government and administration.

Power shifts

By traveling, acquiring wealth, and perpetuating a demand for their goods and services, merchants, craftworkers, and those who offered valuable services to the community became more prestigious. A new class, the **middle class,** emerged as a feature of the city. Increasingly, members of the middle class had financial and political power.

Debt, in addition to wealth, was a notable feature of Renaissance society. People began to buy on credit and often carried large debts. Wealthy merchants had extra money that they would loan in exchange for interest and some became bankers.

Printing

A printing press was invented by Johannes Gutenberg in 1440. Printing was not new, however. People had found ways to use blocks and other objects to leave images on surfaces. But the printing press had two new elements that were revolutionary.

When books were printed before, each page had to be created on a template. It was a lengthy and difficult process to hand carve each page on a template or stamp. Gutenberg had the idea that he should create multiple stamps of each alphabet letter. Then, each page could be composed using an arrangement of these reusable alphabet stamps.

The printing press made it possible to produce many books and to make them affordably.

Gutenberg did not want anyone to steal his idea, nor did he want to reveal his invention before it was perfect. This was a lengthy process—about twenty years of effort were involved in creating the printing press.

He further improved the printing process by taking the screw press that was used for things such as pressing olive oil from olives and adapting it to make it possible to create an even pressure on a typeset page.
In this way, he could create many identical pages of uniform quality.

The Gutenberg Bible

The Gutenberg Bible was created on the new printing press. It was made with less expense than earlier books. This meant people who might not have been able to afford an expensive, hand-copied manuscript could finally own a book. More people wanted to learn to read and write as a result.

Paper made from **linen** was inexpensive to make. Because of that, more people could afford the books that were printed on it.

Dante

Dante Alighieri was from Florence. He studied **classical** literature and then wrote it in language that people from his region could understand. He convinced people that their language was beautiful and could be used to express grand ideas. *Divine Comedy* is a famous **epic** that he wrote.

Boccaccio

Boccaccio was a Tuscan who wrote *Decameron*. This is the story of seven women and three men fleeing Florence to escape the **plague** of 1348. While in the countryside, they told tales. Each tale ended with a song. Unlike Dante's *Divine Comedy,* which was based on religious themes, *Decameron* was based on everyday life.

Divine Comedy

Divine Comedy is a long poem that Dante spent thirteen years writing. It is a story about the afterlife in which Dante is the main character. He is wandering through a forest, lost, when the classic poet Virgil leads him on a journey from hell to paradise. At paradise he meets Beatrice, and the poem becomes a love poem for her.

Dante's real first name was Durante. Dante was a nickname.

Chaucer

Geoffrey Chaucer wrote *The Canterbury Tales,* in which people of various lifestyles and social status tell tales while on a **pilgrimage** to the **shrine** of St. Thomas à Becket. Chaucer's book was unique because his characters were not just **nobles** or royalty, nor were they just serfs or peasants. Instead, his characters represented the new **middle class,** as well as everyday people.

The characters in *The Canterbury Tales* came from various backgrounds. The knight is depicted here in a woodcut from one of the earlier versions of the book.

Cervantes

Miguel de Cervantes was born in Spain. When he wrote *Man of la Mancha* he created what some have called the first novel. It was a story about a man named Don Quixote. The book explores Don Quixote's feelings and thoughts.

Shakespeare

William Shakespeare is known for creating plays that explored people's relationships and portrayed humor, tragedy, and romance. People would rush to the theater to see his plays. During the Renaissance, plays relied more on the spoken word than on sets and props. So, people went as much to hear as to see a play.

Shakespeare wrote many of his greatest plays for production at the Globe Theatre in London.

Realism caused those in the field of science to begin examining their world. Much of the knowledge that was shared among doctors was based on theories without diagrams. Doctors were trying to cure injury and disease based on what they thought the body might look like inside, rather than having an accurate, anatomical map.

Galen

Many beliefs about anatomy were based on guessing what was inside the human body or on what was drawn from studies of apes and pigs. Galen, who lived from about 130–200 C.E., was a famous doctor who wrote extensively about medicine. He figured out that arteries carried blood instead of air. He studied anatomy by looking at his

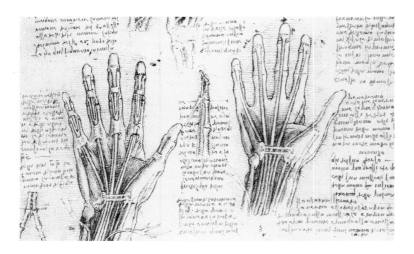

Leonardo da Vinci studied the bodies of dead people and drew diagrams of what he saw in his notebooks. But since his notebooks remained private for many years, he did not further science at the time.

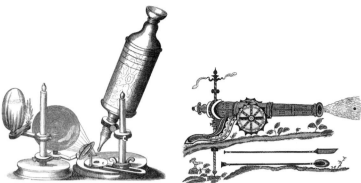

patient's wounds. He assumed that he could draw conclusions about the human body from looking at the internal organs of pigs.

Renaissance medical discoveries

Andreas Vesalius drew diagrams of human bodies. He studied the remains of people who died from accidents, war, disease, and old age. Some people, for religious or other reasons, felt that studying bodies in this way was wrong. However, from his studies, he discovered how the breastbone was actually shaped. He also learned the configuration of the small bones of the ear.

William Harvey figured out how the circulatory system worked by studying the direction that blood flows through the heart. Much of what was discovered about anatomy in the Renaissance forms the foundation of modern medicine.

The invention of the microscope allowed people to see tiny organisms and gave them clues about the cause and cure of disease. Cannons were an invention that aided in warfare. Some people even had more "far-fetched" ideas, like da Vinci's plan for a flying machine.

A War About Science

While new ideas were exciting to many, they made some uncomfortable. Dissecting bodies was furthering scientific knowledge, but some had religious objections to it. Old cures were used alongside new ones to treat illnesses.

Magnetic compass

The magnetic compass was a great help to ship captains as they crossed the sea. The captain would often hide his magnetic compass so as not to disturb his crew. Many thought that the

The magnetic compass was a useful tool for navigating the dangerous ocean. Captains of ships could now be more confident about the direction in which they were sailing.

Galileo created a telescope that could view planets. By the early 1600s he was viewing Jupiter's moons. He used the telescope to prove Copernicus's idea that the planets revolved around the Sun was right.

compass worked by magic. They did not understand that its properties came naturally from a mineral found in the ground.

Stars and planets

As scientists turned their attention to stars and planets, new controversies arose. Copernicus was jailed for his idea that the planets revolved around the Sun and not the Earth. Copernicus, a Polish astronomer, published a book promoting his idea. The Catholic Church banned the book because it was felt that God had put the Earth at the center of the universe.

Patrons and Art

Patrons

If a person hoped to make a living as an artist, it was necessary to find a **patron.** A patron was a wealthy person or family that supported the arts by purchasing and sometimes commissioning works. There was much competition to own art. Wealthy people and heads of churches competed because good art was not only nice to look at, but also a status symbol. An artist could make a living if they caught the attention of just such a person.

Young artists learned to grind their own **pigments** for paint and used models to perfect their drawing skills.

The Catholic Church was one of the largest patrons of the arts. This piece of embroidery depicts the birth of Christ.

Art and the Church

Patrons were not always private individuals and families. Churches were often highly decorated and had many resources to spend on art. So, some artists found the Church to be their patron and their art focused on portraying biblical stories and ideas.

The Vatican is full of art. The paintings on the Sistine Chapel, done by Michelangelo, show the story of creation. Lorenzo Ghiberti portrayed Bible scenes on bronze doors for a Florence **cathedral's baptistery.** The north doors alone took 21 years to complete. Michelangelo called them "the doors of paradise."

Leonardo da Vinci

Leonardo da Vinci was an artist and inventor. He wanted to know all he could about everything. He loved and studied nature. He was **apprenticed** in the workshop of painter and sculptor Andrea del Verrocchio.

At the age of 25, Leonardo had his own studio and was supporting himself with commissions. When he was 30, he went to Milan and stayed there for 18 years.

Leonardo studied anatomy, biology, mathematics, physics, and mechanics. He collected fossils and dissected corpses to learn how the body was designed. He came up with ways to use canals and dams to reconfigure waterways in times of war. He suggested that a tent-like structure could be attached to a person as a parachute and he drew aircraft modeled after birds and bats. Planes and parachutes would not be used with even minimal success until the early 1900s. Leonardo had envisioned these inventions long before anyone else actually built working models.

The *Mona Lisa* is one of the few existing paintings by Leonardo da Vinci.

Leonardo's notebooks are full of designs for flying machines, parachutes, and weapons. Almost all of his notebooks were written in backwards mirror writing.

Michelangelo

Michelangelo Buonarroti was another famous artist. He was a **perfectionist.** He considered himself a sculptor rather than a painter. Even so, he was commissioned to paint the Sistine Chapel, which he accepted out of devotion to the Church. One of his most beautiful works of art is painted on the ceiling. He worked through backache and eyestrain for four years. His clothes were so filthy that they began to rot on his body. However, he certainly must have known how important his work was, because he continued and people can still see his amazing work today.

This is a section of the ceiling at the Sistine Chapel in Rome.

Michelangelo was also an architect. He was a typical Renaissance man—he could do many things well.

In the Renaissance, mapmakers tried to translate flat maps into the first globe. A globe from 1492 shows only Europe, Africa, and Asia. If a mapmaker did not know anything about a certain area, he would decorate it with imaginary countries and creatures.

Europeans received a lot of new information about what the world was really like during the Renaissance. But gathering that information was a difficult job for explorers. The ocean was large and weather was often rough. Navigational instruments were simple. A large sandglass was used to tell how much time had passed. Inventors worked to find a time-keeping device other than the pendulum and sandglass that could work on the tossing and turning waves. A captain studied the sky, watched the forming of clouds, and watched how birds were flying to orient himself. He also could use his magnetic compass.

Christopher Columbus

Most Renaissance exploration was motivated by the quest for better **trade** routes. In 1492, Christopher Columbus set out on a westward

The astrolabe, an ancient instrument, helped explorers determine the position of the sun and other heavenly bodies. This helped them chart their course.

The magnetic compass made it easier for explorers to find their way.

Renaissance explorers had to plan their travels using only the information available at the time. Many maps were not very accurate. The astronomer Ptolemy had underestimated the size of the earth, which is part of the reason Columbus thought he had reached India.

voyage to find a new trade route to India. When he finally did reach land, he brought new information to mapmakers in Europe. It did take a while, though, to clear up his belief that he was in India. Back in Europe, Columbus received a lot of attention for his discovery.

Other explorers

Other explorers, like Bartholomeu Diaz and Vasco de Gama brought new information to Europe as they explored the coast of Africa and looked for a route to India. Ferdinand Magellan sailed around the world. Hernando Cortes landed on the coast of Mexico, where he encountered the Aztecs.

Trade and Trade Routes

Merchants and trade

A network of **trade** routes criss-crossed Europe and the Mediterranean Sea. In major cities, there were places for **merchants** to stay and places to safely store their goods. Eventually, merchants employed others to market their goods and oversee their interests abroad. Meanwhile, they developed more sophisticated business practices such as the sale of stock, accounting systems, credit finance, and international banking.

Merchant ships used the sea to carry their goods abroad. This painting shows the busy Renaissance port of Genoa.

This trade caravan is traveling through central Asia. Europeans learned how to make silk from the Chinese, who they contacting through trade.

Changing trade

Increased interest and competition in trade motivated explorers and discoverers. Europeans also adjusted their economy with changing times. When grain fell in price, they switched to an economy based on the sale of wine, oil, and cheese. They traded silk as exports of wool declined and they specialized in artistic luxuries such as metalwork and furniture when they were in demand.

Weapons and Warfare

Despite the amazing intellect and artistic creativity of the Renaissance, people were still not beyond the daily struggles of warfare. **City-states** came into conflict with each other over issues such as who should control particular trade routes or what the official boundary of each city-state actually was. Each side would argue for the routes and boundaries that were advantageous to them. Spies kept track of what others were planning.

Portable cannons with rocket-like missiles were designed for use in battle.

Battles were common. Citizens of a city were expected to fight for their city. The rich were expected to obtain armor for themselves and advance the battle on horses. They charged

Even horses were trained for battle—they were taught to kick backwards during battle. This painting shows the Battle of San Romano in 1432.

Weapons used during the Renaissance included the mace, sword, crossbow, and harquebus. People would bring whatever they had to fight with into battle.

forward with horses rather than on foot, because they could afford horses. Citizens who could not afford armor and horses served as the infantry.

Sieges of cities and towns were generally long. These battles could last years, with no true winner. A treaty was often the only way to end a war.

The crossbow was a common weapon in the early Renaissance. The harquebus was a type of gun that replaced the crossbow, but had poor aim. People would often bring their own swords or **maces** with them into battle.

Mercenaries

Though fighting was common, people often found themselves too busy with their **trade** activities to fight. They began to hire mercenaries to fight in their place. Whole cities would even hire a commander, who would bring in a professional army to protect the city. When faced with certain loss, many commanders would surrender rather than lose their men. Commanders could hire their army out to another city and continue to earn a living, rather than be killed on the job.

The Renaissance in Europe

The Renaissance lives on in Europe. Buildings and artwork from the time remain. Scientific instruments and medical drawings have also survived. Pages from Leonardo da Vinci's notebooks, engravings, and printed books are a connection to the past. But, more has survived than just artifacts. The Renaissance created a new way of life. Artists took a place of importance within society and their imaginations were turned loose by the techniques and ideas of the Renaissance. In a similar fashion, scientists, **theologians,** writers, **merchants,** and politicians today use ideas and inventions that were first thought of during the Renaissance.

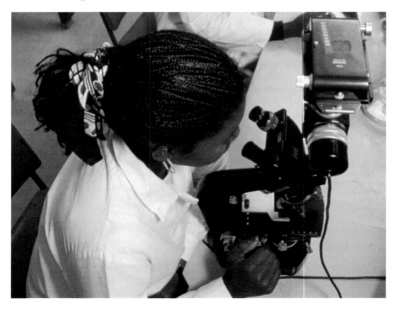

The microscope is a Renaissance invention. Today, the microscope has multiple uses in science, technology, and medicine.

The invention of the printing press changed the world forever. For the first time, books were available to all who wished to have them. We have since improved on the printing press, but the general idea behind the invention remains the same.

The Renaissance around the world

The Renaissance has grown beyond Europe. The viewpoints of the Renaissance have crossed many geographic boundaries. Around the world, people have been influenced by the accomplishments of the Renaissance. The emergence of a **middle class** economy in Renaissance Europe has also ushered in our modern age of commerce, banking, investing, and building businesses. Just as Renaissance glass artists found a way to make windows from panes of glass to let in more light, the Renaissance has lit the way for the achievements of modern times.

Time Line

1283	The magnetic compass is invented.
1307–1321	Dante writes the *Divine Comedy.*
1348	**Plague** drastically reduces the European population.
1353	*Decameron* is published.
1381	English peasants revolt.
1387–1390	Chaucer writes *The Canterbury Tales.*
1402	Ghiberti wins contest to design **baptistery** doors.
1420–1436	Filippo Brunelleschi plans and builds dome in Florence.
1423	Vittorino da Feltre opens Mantua school.
1432	Battle of San Romano.
1434	The Medici family is powerful in Florence.
1440	Gutenberg invents his printing press.
1447–1455	**Pope** Nicholas V increases the number of volumes of ancient Greek books in the Vatican Library from 3 to 350.
1452	Leonardo da Vinci is born.
1453	End of the Hundred Years War that began during the **Middle Ages. Turks** invade Constantinople.
1455	The Gutenberg Bible is printed.
1475	Birth of Michelangelo.
1492	Columbus sails across the Atlantic. Martin Behain makes the first globe map of the world.
1495–1497	da Vinci paints *The Last Supper.*
1500s	Invention of the harquebus.
1501–1504	Michelangelo sculpts statue of David.

1503	da Vinci paints the *Mona Lisa.*
1506	*Laocoon* is discovered.
1508–1512	Michelangelo paints the ceiling of the Sistine Chapel.
1519–1521	Magellan sails around the world.
1534	Luther's Bible is published. Henry VIII breaks with Rome and declares himself head of the Church of England.
1543	Copernicus publishes theory that planets revolve around the Sun, not around the Earth.
1564	William Shakespeare is born.
1567	The first theater is built in London, England.
1584	Sir Walter Raleigh founds the first English colony in Virginia.
1588–1611	Shakespeare writes most of his plays.
1590	Zacharias Jansen invents the microscope.
1599	The original Globe Theatre is built.
1607	John Smith founds the Jamestown colony in Virginia.
1610	Galileo improves the telescope design and writes a book stating that the Earth moves around the Sun.
1618	Weekly newspapers appear in Europe.
1620	Pilgrims sail to North America aboard the *Mayflower.*
1633	Galileo is taken before an Inquisition in Rome, and is forced to deny that the Earth moves around the Sun.

Glossary

agricultural related to raising crops or animals

apprentice young person learning the trade or skill of an expert

archaeology study of past people and cultures

baptistery part of church used for baptism

cathedral home church of a bishop

city-state politically independent city

classic relating to the ancient Greeks or Romans and their culture

clergy ordained members of a church, such as priests, nuns, and monks

commercial pertaining to the sale of goods and services

convent place where female clergy train and live

culture way of life

democracy form of government in which leaders are chosen by the people

diplomat person who works to keep good relations between governments of different countries

epic long story, usually about a hero or heroic event

excavation place where archaeologists dig to find out about the past

feudal system system by which poorer people lived on richer people's land in exchange for some sort of service

fortification part of a building that helps protect the people inside

fox and geese game similar to tag in which the "fox" tries to catch the "geese"

fresco style of painting whereby pictures are created on wet plaster and become a permanent part of the wall

grammar study of what is correct to use in speaking and writing

guild organization in which membership is based upon a particular craft, trade, or occupation

Holy Roman Empire German-based empire in western and central Europe that lasted from 962 C.E. to 1806 C.E.

linen fabric made from plant fiber

mace heavy war club with a spiked head

merchant person who buys goods in one place and sells them in another, often in a different country

Middle Ages name given to the time between classic and modern history, about 476 C.E. to 1492 C.E.

middle class social group consisting of people who are neither rich nor poor

mural large painting on a wall or ceiling

mythology collection of legends that tell of people with special powers or events that cannot be explained

nine men's morris game like tic-tac-toe where players try to get three pieces in a row

noble person born into an important family; a man of noble rank was sometimes called a *nobleman*

opaque hard to see through

palazzo mansion

Pantheon domed, circular temple in Rome

parchment paper-like sheet made from animal skin

patron person who financially supports an artist

perfectionist person who works on something until they believe it is perfect

pigment colorful substance, usually used when painting

pilgrimage journey to a holy place, often as an act of devotion

plague destructive, epidemic disease

pope leader of the Catholic Church

prior elder or superior in a religious order

Protestant member of a Christian church other than the Eastern Orthodox Church and the Roman Catholic Church

realism seeing things as they are and reproducing them artistically in a way close to how they actually appear

reform to make better or improve

restorer person who returns something to its original state

rhetoric art of using language

Roman Empire lands and people under the rule of ancient Rome

scholar person who knows a lot about one or more subjects

shrine place devoted to honoring a saint or holy person

solder to join together using heated metal

theology study of religion

trade to buy and sell goods

Turk native of Turkey, person who speaks Turkish, or a person of Turkish descent

tutor teacher who is hired for private instruction

More Books to Read

Netzley, Patricia D. *Life During the Renaissance.* Farmington Hills, Mich.: Gale Group, 1997.

Proctor, Paul. *The Renaissance.* Columbus, Ohio: McGraw-Hill Children's Publishing, 2000.

Reid, Struan. *Christopher Columbus.* Chicago: Heinemann Library, 2002.

Index